D1192622

Meet my neighbor, the

firefighter

Marc Crabtree
Author and Photographer

🌱 Crabtree Publishing Company
www.crabtreebooks.com

☘ Crabtree Publishing Company

Meet my neighbor, the firefighter

For Ruth Lancashire, with thanks

Author and photographer
Marc Crabtree

Editorial director
Kathy Middleton

Editor
Crystal Sikkens

Design
Katherine Berti
Samantha Crabtree

Print and production coordinator
Katherine Berti

Photographs
All photographs by Marc Crabtree except:
Shutterstock: pages 3, 24 (fire truck, fire station, hydrant)
Wikimedia Commons: Skipatrolkid: page 24 (Halligan bar-top); Derek Eiland: page 24 (Halligan bar-bottom)

Library and Archives Canada Cataloguing in Publication

Crabtree, Marc
    Meet my neighbor, the firefighter / Marc Crabtree, author and photographer.

(Meet my neighbor)
Issued also in electronic format.
ISBN 978-0-7787-0872-8 (bound).--ISBN 978-0-7787-0876-6 (pbk.)

    1. Lancashire, Ruth--Juvenile literature. 2. Fire fighters--Biography--Juvenile literature. 3. Fire extinction--Juvenile literature.
I. Title. II. Series: Crabtree, Marc Meet my neighbor.

TH9118.L36C73 2013   j363.37092   C2013-900130-1

Library of Congress Cataloging-in-Publication Data

CIP available at Library of Congress

Crabtree Publishing Company

www.crabtreebooks.com   1-800-387-7650

Printed in Canada/012013/MA20121217

Published in Canada
Crabtree Publishing
616 Welland Ave.
St. Catharines, Ontario
L2M 5V6

Published in the United States
Crabtree Publishing
PMB 59051
350 Fifth Avenue, 59th Floor
New York, New York 10118

Published in the United Kingdom
Crabtree Publishing
Maritime House
Basin Road North, Hove
BN41 1WR

Published in Australia
Crabtree Publishing
3 Charles Street
Coburg North
VIC, 3058

Contents

Meet my Neighbor

Meet my neighbor, Ruth Lancashire, and her dog, Jasper. Ruth is a firefighter.

Firefighters are important people. They put out fires in buildings, forests, and cars. They also rescue people that are trapped by a fire.

Ruth begins her day at the **fire station**. This is where the **fire trucks** and equipment are kept. She helps Wade wash and clean a fire truck. They are making sure it is clean and ready for the next emergency.

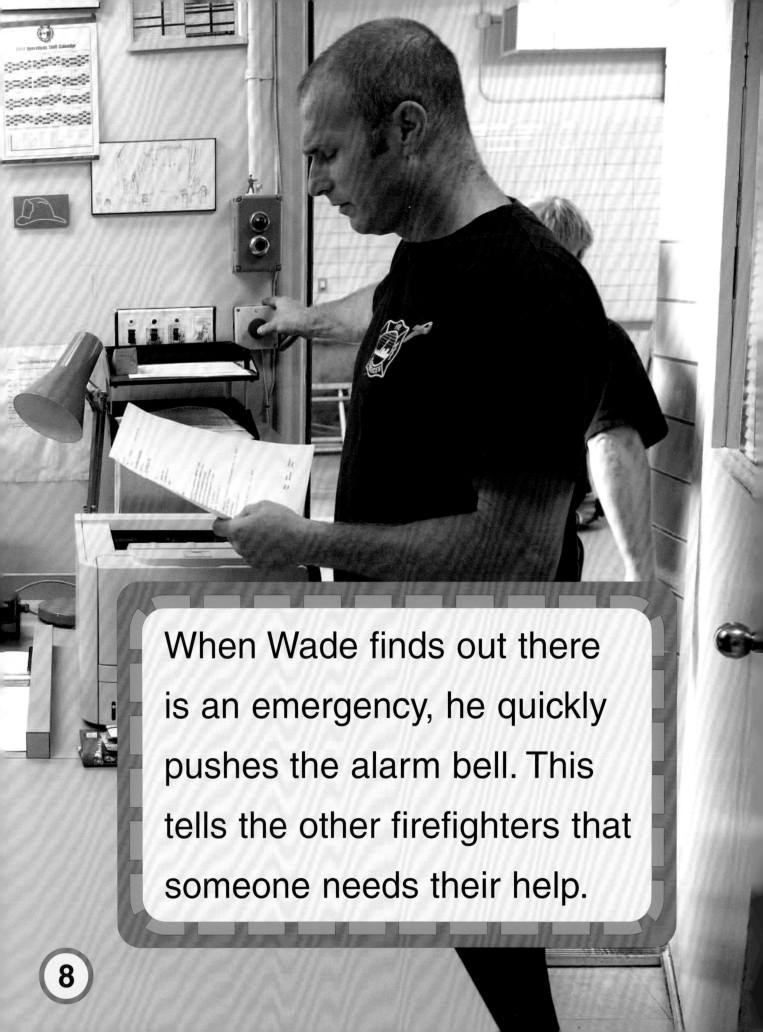

When Wade finds out there is an emergency, he quickly pushes the alarm bell. This tells the other firefighters that someone needs their help.

When Ruth hears the alarm, she uses a **firepole** to get to the bottom floor of the fire station fast. Using the firepole is quicker than using the stairs.

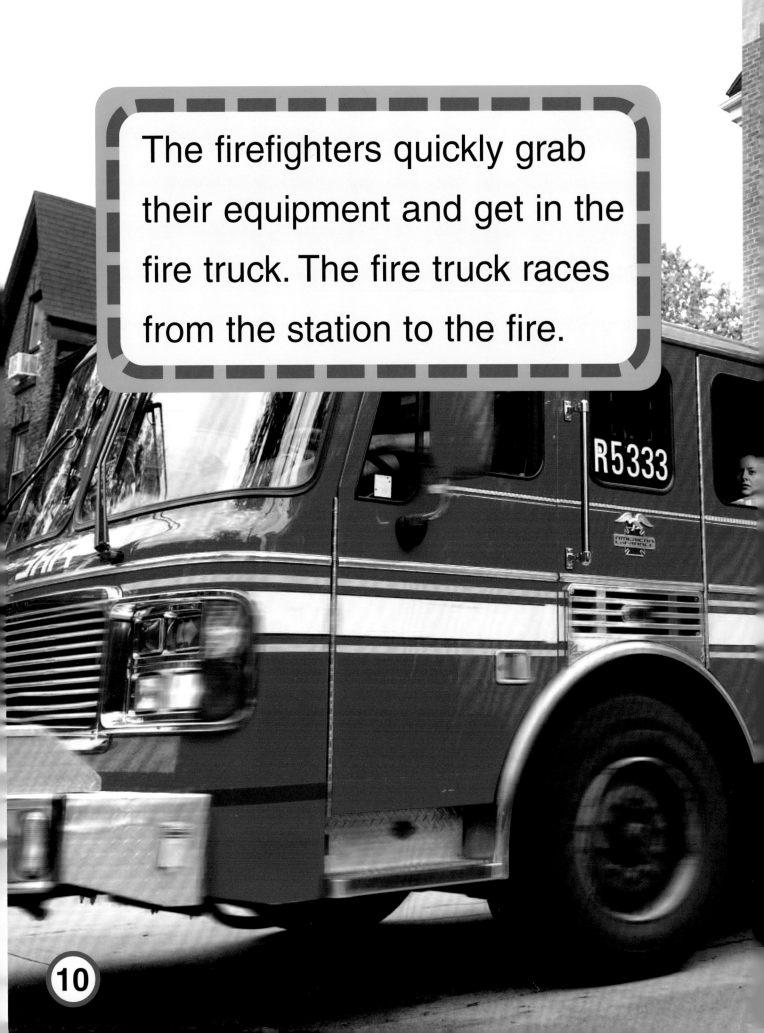

The firefighters quickly grab their equipment and get in the fire truck. The fire truck races from the station to the fire.

FIRE STATION · № 23 ·

FIRE
911

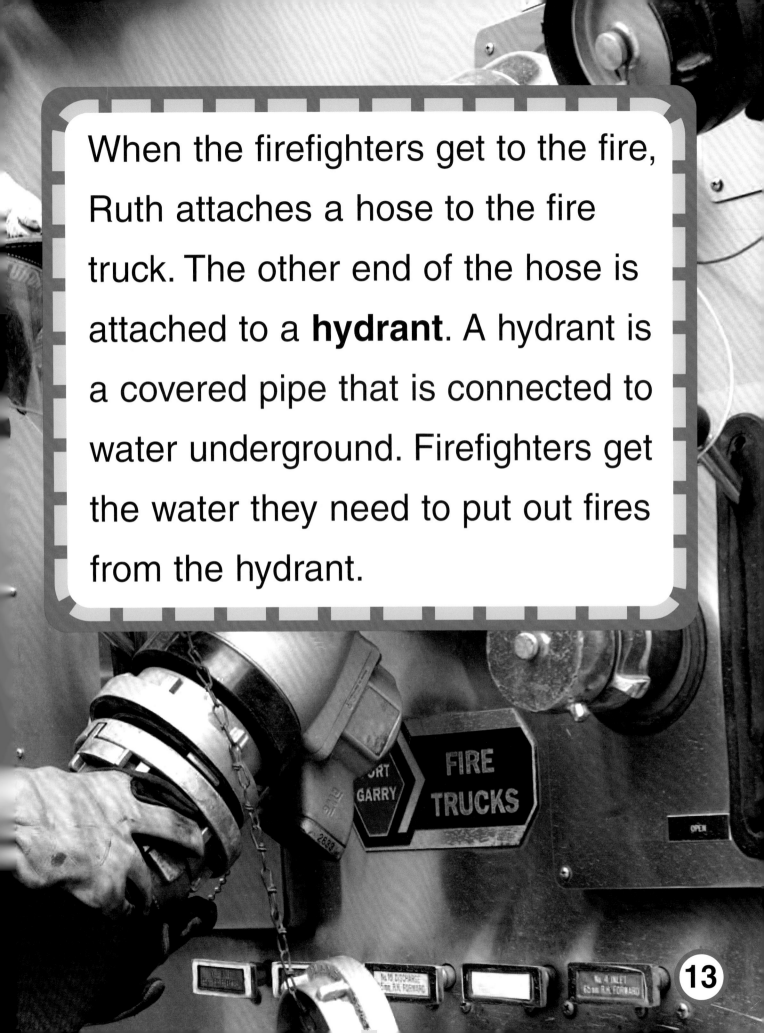

When the firefighters get to the fire, Ruth attaches a hose to the fire truck. The other end of the hose is attached to a **hydrant**. A hydrant is a covered pipe that is connected to water underground. Firefighters get the water they need to put out fires from the hydrant.

hydrant

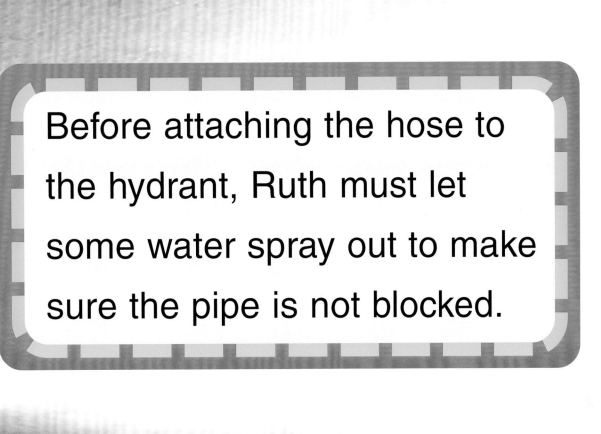

Before attaching the hose to the hydrant, Ruth must let some water spray out to make sure the pipe is not blocked.

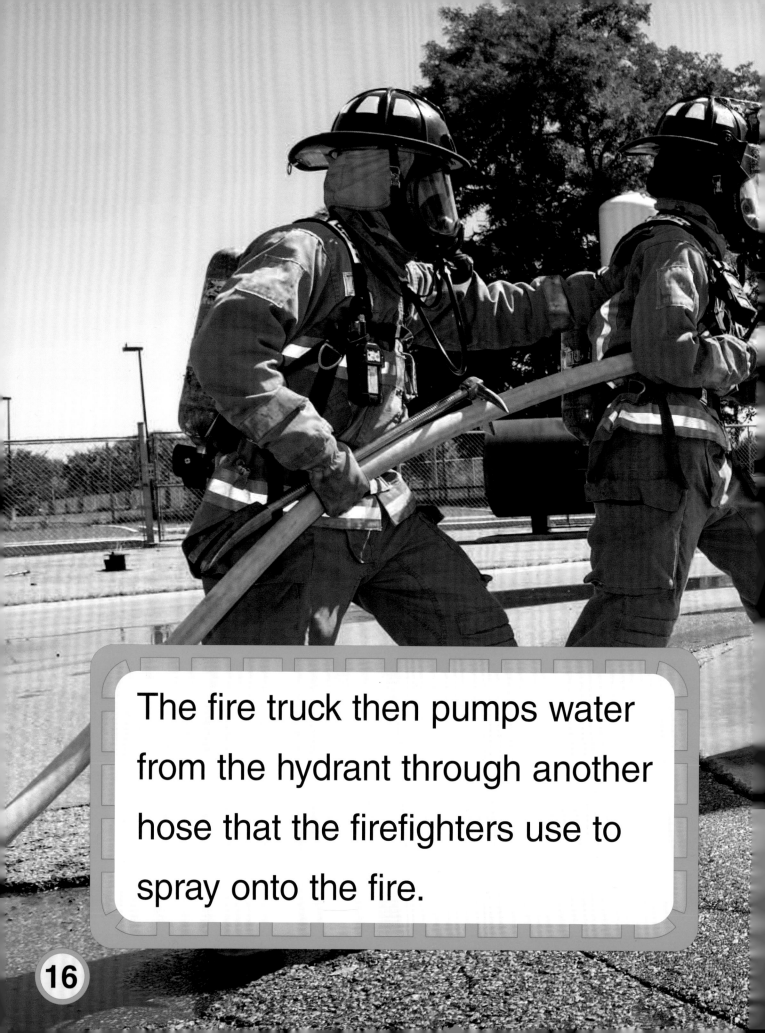

The fire truck then pumps water from the hydrant through another hose that the firefighters use to spray onto the fire.

The fire hose is very heavy and a lot of water sprays out of the hose at once. Jost helps Ruth carry the hose and aim the water at the fire.

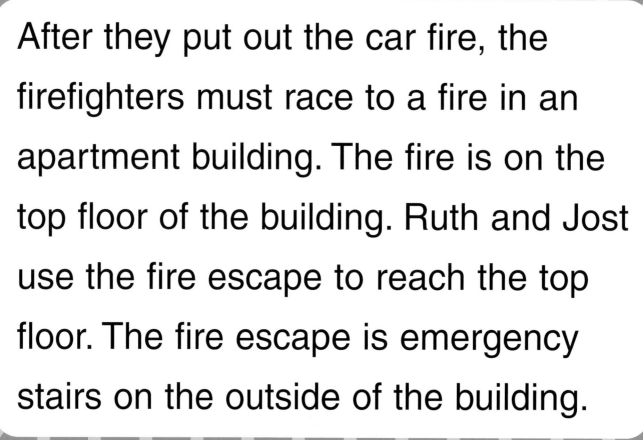

After they put out the car fire, the firefighters must race to a fire in an apartment building. The fire is on the top floor of the building. Ruth and Jost use the fire escape to reach the top floor. The fire escape is emergency stairs on the outside of the building.

Before entering the building, Ruth and Jost put on special breathing equipment. This helps them breathe clean air instead of the smoke from the fire.

Ruth and Jost carry the hose to the room that is on fire. Ruth feels the door before entering the room. If the door is hot, she knows the flames from the fire are on the other side.

Once the door is open, smoke rushes from the room. Before they enter, Ruth makes sure the floor is still strong enough to hold them. For this, she uses a special tool called a **Halligan bar**.

Ruth and Jost worked hard to put out the fire. They both made it out safely.

Firefighters risk their own lives to help others. Even though it is dangerous, Ruth and her friends love their job!

Glossary

fire escape

firepole

fire station

fire truck

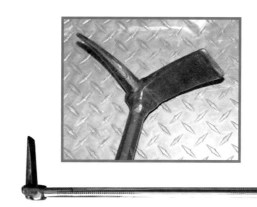

Halligan bar

hydrant